THE LIFE OF
Jesus

Published by
Christian Focus Publications Ltd

Tain   Houston
Ross-shire Texas

© Christian Focus Publications 1990

ISBN 0 906731 89 5

Illustrations by Morna Whyte

Text by Carine MacKenzie
Design and layout by Creative Link of Dalgety Bay

CONTENTS

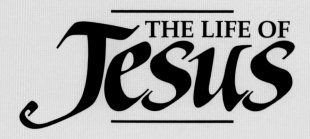
THE LIFE OF Jesus

LOOKING FORWARD TO HIS COMING

Jewish boys and girls, who lived many years before Jesus was born, were taught the words of the Old Testament. They knew the books of Moses; they sang the Psalms; they heard the words of the prophets like Isaiah. They knew that one day God would send the Messiah to save His people.

They would read in the first book of the Old Testament, Genesis, that a man would be born who would have victory over sin and Satan. **(Genesis 3.15)**

They would know about Abraham who was told that this man who would be such a blessing to all nations would be one of his descendants. **(Genesis 18.18)**

They would have read in the book of Isaiah that this man would come from the family of Jesse, the father of the great King David. **(Isaiah 11.1)**

They would have discovered in Isaiah a very amazing sign to look out for. 'A virgin shall conceive and bear a son and shall call His name Immanuel (God with us).' **(Isaiah 7.14)**

The Messiah who was promised would be no ordinary man. He was God who would in a very extraordinary way take a truly human body yet still be truly God.

If they read the book of the prophet Micah they would find out where He was to be born, - in the little town of Bethlehem.

(Micah 5.2)

God's people were given these promises - some very early in the history of the World.

Why did Jesus come into the world?

1

IMMANUEL - GOD WITH US

Mary the mother of Jesus was a young Jewish woman, engaged to be married to Joseph. She lived in the city of Nazareth in Galilee. The angel called Gabriel was sent to Mary with a message from God.

He greeted her. 'Hail to you. You are highly favoured. The Lord is with you. Blessed are you among women.'

Mary was anxious about this visit. She could not understand at all.

'Do not be afraid, Mary,' the angel added, 'you have found favour with God. You will conceive and give birth to a son and shall call His name Jesus. He shall be a great king, the Son of the Highest.'

Mary was amazed. 'How can this happen? I am not married yet.'

'The Holy Spirit shall come upon you,' the angel replied, 'the power of God shall overshadow you. The holy child whom you shall bear will be the Son of God'.

Mary humbly acknowledged this wonderful fact. 'Behold the handmaid of the Lord,' she said. 'May what happens to me be according to your word.'

The angel left her.

Mary soon made a journey to the hill country of Judea to visit her cousin Elisabeth. Elisabeth was old but she was expecting a baby herself in three months time. (Her baby would grow up to be John the Baptist, a great preacher who would tell people that they would soon see Jesus).

As soon as Mary entered the house, the baby inside Elisabeth moved vigorously.

Elisabeth was filled with the Holy Spirit and called out loudly, 'Blessed are you among women and blessed is the child that you are bearing. Why has the mother of my Lord come to visit me?'

Mary then spoke words of praise and love to God her Saviour, for His goodness and mercy to her even although she was a poor woman.

After staying with Elisabeth for about three months, Mary went home to Nazareth.

When it became known that Mary was expecting a baby, Joseph to whom he was engaged, was rather perplexed about what to do.

An angel appeared to him in a dream. 'Joseph, son of David,' the angel said, 'do not be afraid to take Mary as your wife, for her child was conceived by the power of the Holy Spirit. She will give birth to a son and you will call His name Jesus: for He shall save His people from their sins.'

Would Joseph have remembered what was written in the book of the prophet Isaiah about the Messiah being born of a virgin?

Joseph was reassured and he took Mary to be his wife and he looked after her.

2
GOOD TIDINGS OF GREAT JOY

Caesar Augustus, the Emperor, passed a law that everyone in his Empire should be taxed. Each man had to return to his home town to be enrolled.

Joseph belonged to the family of David so he had to go to Bethlehem, the city of David. Mary, his wife had to go with him, even although her baby was due very soon.

The town of Bethlehem was very busy with other visitors like Joseph, in town to be taxed. The town was so busy in fact that there was no room left in the inn for Mary and Joseph to sleep overnight. They were given shelter in the stable. While they were there the baby was born. Mary wrapped her baby in swaddling clothes, like a very tight shawl and laid Him to sleep in a manger which would usually hold straw to feed the animals.

That same night some shepherds in the country close by were watching over their flocks of sheep as usual. Suddenly an angel

of the Lord appeared to them. There was a great brightness in the sky showing them the Glory of the Lord. The shepherds were very afraid.

The angel spoke to them. 'Do not be afraid. I am bringing you good news, joyful news for all people. For today in the city of David is born a Saviour who is Christ the Lord. You will find this baby wrapped in swaddling clothes and lying in a manger.'

This angel was then joined by many more and they all praised God saying, 'Glory to God in the Highest, and on earth peace, good will toward men.'

When the angels returned to heaven, the shepherds turned to one another and said, 'Let's go to Bethlehem and see for ourselves this wonderful thing that the Lord has told us.'

So they hurried to Bethlehem and found Mary and Joseph, with the baby lying in the manger. It was just as the angels had said.

The shepherds passed on this joyful news to as many people as they could, 'The Saviour, Christ the Lord, has been born in Bethlehem,' they exclaimed.

They returned to their work in the fields glorifying and praising God for the good news that they had heard and the proof of these words which they had seen.

3
TAKEN TO THE TEMPLE

When Jesus was eight days old, He was brought to the temple at Jerusalem to be presented to the Lord. It was part of the law of Moses that the firstborn boy of every family was to be called 'holy to the Lord'. The parents had to present a sacrifice in the temple. Those who could afford it gave a lamb but Mary and Joseph were poor. They brought a pair of turtledoves or two young pigeons.

In Jerusalem, at that time, lived a good, old man called Simeon. He was upright and holy and was waiting for Christ the Saviour to come. The Holy Spirit had revealed to him that he would not die until he had seen the Lord's anointed one, Jesus Christ. The Holy Spirit prompted him to go to the temple on the same day that Mary and Joseph brought the child Jesus.

Simeon took the baby Jesus in his arms and

praised God. 'Lord, now let Your servant die in peace according to Your Word,' he said, 'for my eyes have seen Your salvation, which you have prepared to save both Jews and Gentiles.'

Joseph and Mary were amazed at the words spoken by Simeon.

Simeon blessed them and spoke particularly to Mary. 'This child,' he said, 'is come as a Saviour for many in Israel but those who reject Him will fall. You too will have your own share of suffering.'

An old widow of about eighty four years, called Anna, lived in the temple all the time. She spent day and night praying and fasting. When she saw the baby Jesus, she gave thanks to God. She spoke of Him to many people who were looking for the Saviour. She too believed that Jesus was the Messiah who was promised long before.

4
WISE MEN FROM THE EAST

Wise men from the East were told about the wonderful event of Christ's birth. They studied the stars and one night they saw a special star in the sky.

'The King of the Jews has been born. Let us go to worship Him,' they said.

So they set off on their long journey from the east to the city of Jerusalem and made their way to King Herod's palace.

'Where is the newborn King of the Jews? We have seen His star. We want to worship Him.'

Herod was very upset by this news. He did not want another king to usurp his place. He called the chief priests and scribes together.

'Where will Christ, the Messiah, be born?' he asked.

They remembered the passage in the book of the prophet Micah.

'Christ will be born in Bethlehem,' they told him.

Herod passed on this information to the wise men from the east.

'Look carefully for the young child' he said, 'and tell me where He is so that I too can go to worship Him.'

This was really a wicked plot.

The wise men travelled on to Bethlehem, the special star guiding them all the way and stopping over the house where Jesus was. When they went into the house and saw the young child Jesus and Mary His mother, they fell down and worshipped Him. They gave Him beautiful gifts of gold, frankincense and myrrh.

God warned the wise men in a dream not to go near Herod on the return journey, so they went home by a different route.

Jesus was the Saviour of the world, not just for the Jewish people. The wise men who were foreigners could also worship the Lord.

14

5

THE ESCAPE ROUTE

After the wise men had left to travel home, Joseph had a dream in which an angel spoke to him.

'Take the young child and Mary His mother and go quickly to Egypt. Stay there until I tell you. Herod the King is looking for the young child in order to kill Him .'

So Joseph got up in the middle of the night and immediately, with Mary and the baby, started off on the long journey to Egypt. The family stayed in that country until Herod was dead and that danger was past. Even this small detail was foretold by the prophet Hosea long before. 'Out of Egypt I have called My Son.'

God's Word is true in every detail. When Herod realised that the wise men had tricked him and had not returned to tell him the whereabouts of the 'King of the Jews', he was very angry.

He sent out his men to Bethlehem and all the area round about and they cruelly killed all the babies and young children of two years old and under. What a dreadful thing to do! What grief and sadness would be in so many homes! Herod thought his throne would not be challenged because he was sure that the special baby was bound to be among those killed. But Jesus was safe in Egypt.

After Herod died, the angel of the Lord again spoke to Joseph in a dream.

'Take the young child and His mother back to Israel. The people who wanted to kill Him are now dead!'

With this reassurance Joseph, Mary and the baby made the long journey back to Israel. Archelaus, Herod's son was now King in Judea. Joseph was unhappy about staying there. God warned him again in a dream so they travelled on north to Galilee and settled in the city of Nazareth. Joseph worked there as a carpenter. Jesus grew up strong in spirit and full of wisdom and the grace of God.

6
IN HIS FATHER'S HOUSE

The feast of the Passover was a very important occasion for Jewish families. Every year Joseph and Mary would make the journey from Nazareth to Jerusalem to celebrate this feast in the temple.

When Jesus was twelve years old, He was old enough to go with them. They were there for several days worshipping God. When it was time to set off for home, Jesus stayed behind in the temple, unknown to His parents. Mary and Joseph travelled on assuming that Jesus was in the company of friends, all on the road to Nazareth.

At the end of the day they began to search for Him, asking all their relations and friends, 'Have you seen Jesus? Is He with you?'

The replies were all the same. 'No, we have not seen Him at all today.'

Mary and Joseph anxiously hurried back to Jerusalem looking for Him all the time.

Three days later they found Him in the temple. He was sitting with the learned men, listening to them and asking them questions.

Everyone was astonished at His understanding and at the answers He gave.

When Mary and Joseph saw what He wa doing they were amazed too.

'Son, why did You do this?' cried Mary 'Your father and I have been very worried looking for You.'

Jesus said to them, 'Why were you looking for Me? Did you not know that I have to do My Father's business?'

By this He meant that He needed to be discussing and learning about the things o God, His heavenly Father.

Mary and Joseph did not understand bu Mary remembered these words and though about them often.

Jesus left the wise doctors in the temple a Jerusalem and went home with His parents.

He was a dutiful and obedient son, honouring His father and mother as the law of God commands. There was no sin in Him at all.

As Jesus grew up to be a man, He became [e]ven wiser. God was pleased with His life and [th]e people who came in contact with Him day [b]y day saw that He was a special person.

THE LIFE OF Jesus

LOOKING FORWARD TO HIS WORK

Years before Jesus was born, boys and girls who listened to the words of Isaiah the prophet could learn about how Jesus the Saviour would work.

He would be full of wisdom and understanding and knowledge.

(Isaiah 11.2)

He would be quiet and gentle.

(Isaiah 42.2)

He would be a good shepherd to His people. **(Isaiah 40.11)**

What did Jesus do while He was on earth ?

7

PLEASING HIS FATHER

When Jesus was about thirty years of age, it was time for Him to begin the great work that God had sent Him to do.

He made His way from His home town, Nazareth to the banks of the River Jordan near Bethabara. Many people gathered at this place to hear a special preacher called John, Elisabeth's son.

John told the people, 'You must turn from your sins to God.'

He also told them, 'Someone far mor important will speak to you soon.'

The 'more important' person was Jesus.

One day when Jesus walked towards John John turned to the people and said, 'Behold th Lamb of God that takes away the sin of th world.'

John realised that Jesus was not only a mar

but was God's Son. His listeners would all understand well how a lamb was used in their worship as a sacrifice for sin. This man Jesus was to be the great sacrifice for sin.

Many people turned from their sins when they heard John preaching. These people were baptised in the River Jordan. Jesus also asked to be baptised. John could hardly believe his ears.

'How can I baptise You?' he asked. 'You should baptise me.'

John knew that Jesus had no sin in Him, and had no need of having sin washed away. But Jesus insisted. He was baptised just like the other people who loved the Lord God.

God the Holy Spirit came down from heaven in the form of a dove and rested on Jesus.

God the Father spoke these words, 'This is My beloved Son, in whom I am well pleased.'

8

TESTED BY THE DEVIL

God the Son was now ready to begin His work.

For forty days following this wonderful event, Jesus was alone in the wilderness. Wild beasts roamed around. He was tired and hungry as He had eaten no food in these forty days.

Satan spoke to Him tempting Him to do wrong.

'If You are the Son of God, make these stones into bread,' he said.

Jesus knew the Bible well and He lived, obeying God's Word. He quoted a verse from the Bible in reply.

'It is written,' He said, 'Man shall not live by bread alone, but by every word that God says.'

The devil tried again. He took Jesus up to the temple in Jerusalem, to one of the high towers. 'If You are the Son of God,' he said 'throw Yourself down to the ground, for the Bible says that God will send His angels to take care of You.'

Again Jesus quoted the Bible to counter the attacks of Satan.

'It is written,' He said, 'You shall not tempt the Lord your God.'

Once more the devil tried to make Jesus sin. He took Him up to a high mountain and showed Him all the kingdoms of the world down below. How wonderful they looked.

'I will give all these lands to You,' said Satan, 'if You will only fall down and worship me.'

'Go away, Satan,' Jesus replied. 'It is written "You shall worship the Lord your God and you shall serve only Him".'

The devil could do no more. He left Jesus alone then.

9

AT A WEDDING

Jesus and His mother Mary were invited to a wedding in Cana in Galilee. There were many guests at the wedding feast, including the disciples, Jesus' special friends.

In the middle of the meal, Mary came to Jesus and said, 'The wine is finished. There is no more left.'

Jesus answered her, 'Woman, what can I do about that? My time has not come yet.'

But Mary said to the servants, 'Do whatever Jesus tells you.'

In the room were six big stone waterpots used for washing. Each was able to hold about twenty to thirty gallons of water.

Jesus told the servants, 'Fill the waterpots with water.'

The men filled them up to the brim.

Jesus' next order was, 'Draw out a cupful and take it to the man in charge of the feast.'

When the man drank some, he thought it was the best wine he had ever tasted. He had not been aware of the problem and did not know where the wine had come from. But he called the bridegroom and congratulated him on the good wine.

'Most people give the best wine first,' he said, 'and then bring out the poorer, but you have kept the good wine until now.'

The servants who filled the waterpots and drew the wine from them knew that a miracle had been performed that day.

This was the first miracle that Jesus did. This showed to many His power and glory. The disciples believed on Him.

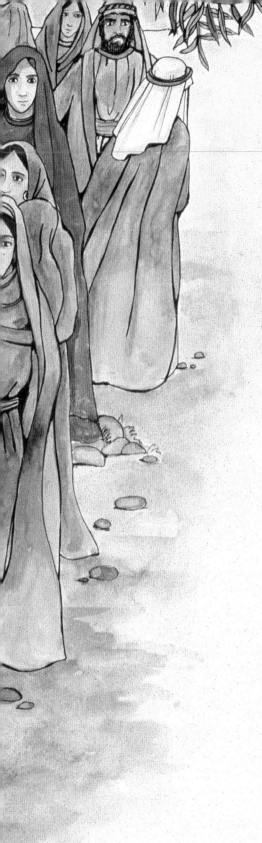

10
RAISING AND HEALING

Jairus was an important man in Capernaum. He was a ruler of the Jewish church, called the synagogue. He was very sad one day. His little girl, only twelve years old, was very ill. He was afraid that she would die.

Jairus had heard about Jesus. Jesus had healed sick people before. He had even raised a boy from the dead.

'If only He would help my daughter,' Jairus thought.

Jairus edged his way through the crowds that pressed on Jesus.

He fell down on his knees before Him and begged Him, 'Please come to my house. My little daughter is so ill. I am afraid she will die.'

Jesus made His way with Jairus towards his house. But so many people crowded round Jesus that it was difficult to make much progress. How hard for Jairus not to feel impatient.

There was a further delay when Jesus suddenly stopped and asked, 'Who touched Me?'

Answers came from all round.

'It wasn't me!' 'No, I didn't touch You either.' 'No, not me.'

Peter and his friends said to Jesus, 'Master, the crowd is so close to You. You should not be surprised that someone has touched You. It could not be avoided.'

Then a woman came out of the crowd. She was afraid and trembling. She fell down in front of Jesus and told her story to Him, with everyone listening.

'I have been ill for twelve years with internal bleeding. I have spent all my money on doctors' bills but not one of them could help me. When I saw You, Jesus, I thought that if I could only touch the hem of Your garment, I might be healed. As soon as I touched, I was healed.'

Jesus comforted and encouraged the woman. He commended her for her faith. Meanwhile

Jairus was standing by waiting for Jesus to come to his house. At that moment, one of Jairus' servants came hurrying up.

'Your daughter is dead,' he said, 'do not trouble the Master.'

But when Jesus heard this He replied, 'Do not be afraid: just believe and she will be made better.'

Jesus and Jairus arrived at the house. There was a large crowd of friends standing around, weeping and making a big fuss. Jesus allowed His special friends Peter, James and John and the mother and father of the little girl to come with Him into the room.

He took the little girl's hand and said, 'Little girl, get up.'

Immediately her life revived, and she got up out of bed. Her mother and father were overjoyed.

'Give her something to eat,' Jesus ordered. 'She will be hungry now.'

Jesus the Creator of Life had power to restore life to the little girl and to heal the woman who had been so ill.

11
A SATISFYING MEAL

John who had baptized Jesus, was cruelly killed on the instruction of a wicked king. Jesus and His disciples were very sad when they heard this tragic news.

'Let's go away to a quiet place,' He said to them, 'and rest for a while. There has been so much happening that we have hardly had time to eat.'

So they sailed off in a little ship across the lake to find a quiet spot to rest.

But someone had seen them go and passed word round the town. So many people wanted to listen to Jesus. They decided to walk round the lake to the spot where Jesus and His friends had reached by boat.

When Jesus saw this large crowd of over 5,000 people He took pity on them and gave up His time of rest in order to speak with them and teach them many things.

When the evening came, the disciples said, 'The day is nearly over. This place is very quiet. There are no shops here, to buy food. Send the people away so that they can go into the villages round about and buy some food for themselves.'

Jesus answered, 'Can you not give them food to eat?'

'Even if we could buy two hundred pence worth of bread,' they replied, 'it would never feed the crowd.'

'Go and find out how many loaves you have,' Jesus said.

'There is a boy here,' replied Andrew, 'who has five small loaves and two little fishes. But how will they feed so many people?'

'Make the people sit down on the grass,' Jesus commanded.

Jesus took the loaves and gave thanks to God for the food. He then broke the loaves and fishes into pieces and handed them to His disciples. They passed the pieces on to the people sitting in groups of fifty or one hundred, on the grass. Jesus kept on breaking the food into pieces until everyone had as much as they could eat.

Jesus the Creator of all food had multiplied the five loaves and two fishes to feed over five thousand people. Afterwards the disciples cleared up what was left. They filled twelve big baskets. Jesus had provided more than enough.

12
SCATTERING THE SEED

One day Jesus went to the shore of the Sea of Galilee. So many people wanted to hear His stories and teaching that He sat in a fishing boat tied up near the shore. The people stood crowded on the beach.

Jesus told a story. A farmer went out to his field to sow some seed. He walked up and down his field scattering the seed from his basket - one handful to the right - one to the left. Some seeds fell on the pathway. The birds soon came and gobbled up the seed. Some seeds fell on shallow stony ground. These seeds grew quickly and soon there was green showing through the earth. But when the sun shone brightly and the day became very hot these shoots withered and died because their roots could not reach down to get moisture.

Other seeds fell among the thorns and weeds. These seeds grew but the thorns grew too and they soon choked the good corn. But some seed also landed on good ground and with no stones or thorns and weeds. This seed grew well and eventually the farmer would harvest his corn reaping perhaps thirty times as much as he planted or even sixty times or even a hundred times as much.

The people would enjoy hearing of this story about something well known to them. But perhaps not everyone would understand the deeper meaning of Jesus' story. He explained the story or parable to His disciples.

The seed is like the Word of God. God sends His Word in different ways to men and women and boys and girls.

Some people hear God's Word but very soon the devil makes them think of something else and forget about the Bible. That is like the seed that fell on the pathway, stolen away by the birds.

Other people hear God's Word and listen to it gladly. It seems to be having an effect on their lives. But when trouble comes, or if someone laughs at them for taking notice of the Bible, their interest in God's Word withers away. They are like the seed sown on stony ground which has no deep root.

Then there was the seed sown among the thorns. What kind of people did Jesus compare to this? They are people who hear the Word of God but riches and pleasures are more important to them and soon any interest in the Bible is choked.

But happily there are some people who hear the Word and love it and obey it. It has a great effect on their lives. Their lives are made new. They believe what is written in the Word and they try to obey what is commanded in the Word.

13

A GOOD NEIGHBOUR

A smart lawyer challenged Jesus one day with a question.

'Master, what shall I do to gain eternal life?'

Jesus replied with another question.

'Well, what do you read in God's Word about that?'

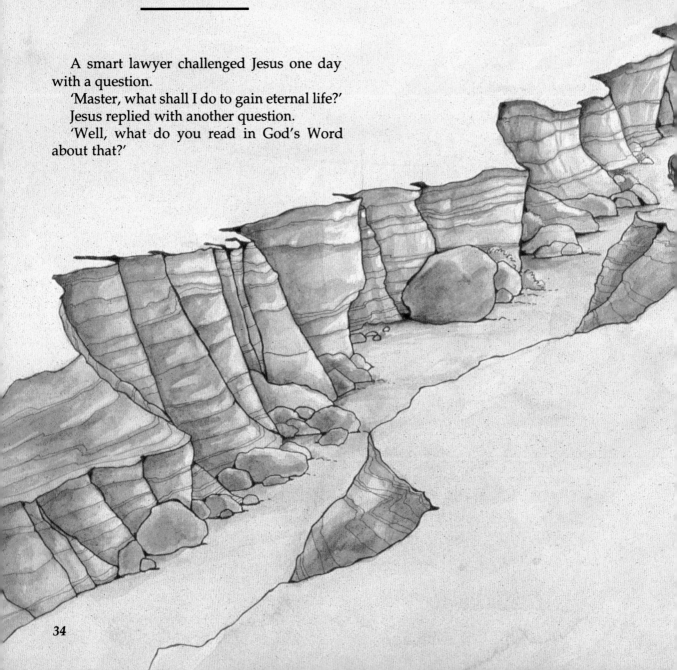

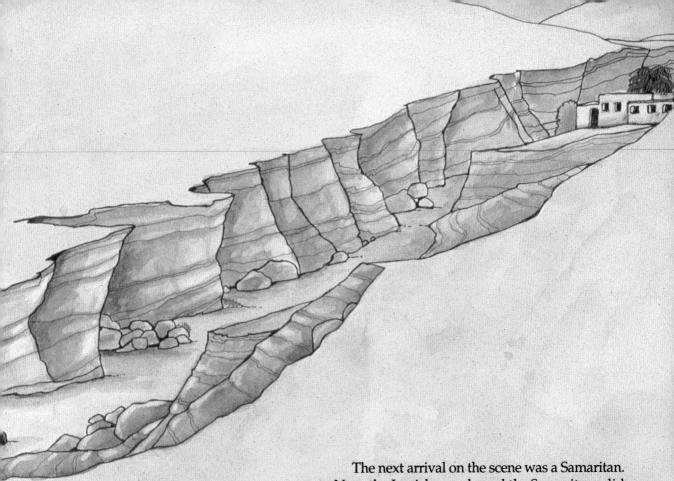

The man answered, 'God's Word tells us to love God with all our heart, soul, strength and mind and also to love our neighbour as ourselves.'

'That is correct,' Jesus replied.

The lawyer added another question.

'But who is my neighbour?'

In answering, Jesus told a story. A man travelled along the dangerous road from Jerusalem to Jericho. A band of thieves pounced on him, stole his clothes, beat him up badly and left him half dead at the roadside. It so happened that a priest was travelling on that road too. He saw the poor man lying naked and battered but he did not even stop to look at him. He hurried on as fast as he could on the other side of the road, showing no love or concern.

The next man to pass along was a Levite, also a churchman. He came up to the man and looked at him. He did not help either. He was too afraid to wait and hurried away on the other side of the road.

The next arrival on the scene was a Samaritan. Now the Jewish people and the Samaritans did not like each other very much. They did not agree on religious matters. Would this man hurry past him too and take nothing to do with the poor injured traveller? No. He took pity on the man. He gave him first aid at the road-side, bandaging up his wounds, and pouring oil and wine on them to soothe and to cleanse the sores. Then he lifted him on to his donkey and they carefully made their way to the nearest inn. There he stayed with the man overnight looking after his needs.

Next day the Samaritan had to leave, but he took the inn keeper aside before he left and said, 'Here is some money. Take care of this man. If you need more than that I will refund you when I pass this way next time.'

Jesus then asked the lawyer the question:

'Which of these three was a neighbour to the man who was attacked?'

The lawyer replied, 'The one who showed kindness to him - the Samaritan.'

So Jesus added, 'You should do the same.'

14

TIME TO CELEBRATE

The church leaders sometimes complained that Jesus spent time with tax collectors and other sinful people. Jesus told some stories to show that there is joy in heaven about one sinner who repents of his sin.

One story was about a father who had two sons. The older son worked at home on his father's farm. The younger son was restless. He wanted to leave home and see the world and have fun.

So one day he said to his father, 'Half of your money, father, will one day be mine. Can I have that money now?'

His father agreed and gave him half of his wealth.

After a few days, the younger son left home and travelled far away. He had plenty of money to spend on clothes and food and parties. He made friends with people who liked him because of his money. But money does not last forever. One day there was no money left. It had all been spent.

At that time there was a shortage of food in the country. The young man was hungry. He needed to find a job. A pig farmer hired him to look after his pigs. The lad was so hungry that he could have eaten the pig's food.

On his own in the field with the pigs, he had time to think seriously.

'Here I am, starving and the lowest servants in my father's house will have plenty to eat. I think I will go back to my father. I will admit that I have sinned against him and against God. I will ask to be one of his servants, for I am not worthy to be his son.'

So he started on his journey back home. When he was still a good distance from his house, he saw a figure running down the road to greet him. It was his father. He welcomed him with open arms, kissed and hugged him.

'Oh father,' the boy said. 'I have done wrong. I have sinned against God and against you. I am not worthy to be your son.'

The father called to his servants. 'Bring out the best robe for my son. Put a ring on his hand and shoes on his feet. Prepare a special meal, with a fat calf. Let's celebrate. My son was as if dead, but now is alive. He was lost and is found.'

What a grand celebration they had. What a home coming.

The older son had been working hard in the fields all day. When he came near the house, he heard the noise of music and dancing.

He shouted to one of the servants, 'What is all this noise about?'

'Oh it is good news,' the servant replied, 'your young brother has come home. Your father is so pleased to have him back safe and sound that he ordered a grand meal, with a fat calf, to celebrate.'

The older brother was so angry that he would not go in to the house. Eventually his father came out and reasoned with him.

But he remained very indignant.

'I have worked for you for years and always done what you wished. Yet you never even gave me a kid, far less a fat calf, to have a party with my friends. But as soon as this boy who has wasted your money comes back, you make a grand feast.'

His Father replied gently, 'Son, you are always with me, and all that I have is yours. It was right for us to rejoice, for your brother was as good as dead but is now alive, he was lost but is now found.'

Jesus was teaching about the love that God has to poor erring sinners. Those who repent and return to God are welcomed with open arms.

THE LIFE OF
Jesus

LOOKING FORWARD TO CALVARY

Children in Zechariah's time heard him tell that their King would ride into Jerusalem on a young ass. **(Zechariah 9.9)**

Isaiah spoke about a man of sorrows, who would be wounded and bruised, yet He would not complain. **(Isaiah 53,5,7)**

David in the book of Psalms told of someone mocked by men **(Psalm 22.7)** betrayed by a friend **(Psalm 41.9)** and given vinegar to drink **(Psalm 69.21)**.

They were all speaking about Jesus and His suffering at Calvary.

Why did Jesus have to die?

15
WHOM DO YOU SAY THAT I AM?

Jesus did many wonderful things. He healed sick people, made blind men see, made deaf people hear, even raised dead people to life again. He taught many wise things to the crowds who followed Him or even to one solitary person who came to Him for help.

Many people believed on Him when they saw the miracles and heard His words. They followed Him and wanted to learn more. Some others did not believe. They liked to see the miracles but they did not believe that Jesus was anyone special. Some of the church leaders were angry that Jesus had such an influence on the people.

One day Jesus and His close friends, the disciples, were talking together in the town of Caesarea Philippi. 'Whom do people say that I am?' asked Jesus.

'Some people think You are John the Baptist, or Elijah, or Jeremiah, or another great prophet come back to life,' they replied.

Then He asked them more personally, 'But whom do you say that I am?'

Simon Peter was the spokesman. 'You are the Christ,' he said, 'the Son of the living God.'

No man told this to Peter, but God had showed him.

From then on Jesus warned His disciples that He would soon have to go to Jerusalem. There He would be killed. He knew that He would suffer a great deal of pain of body and mind. He knew also that not only would He be killed but would rise again on the third day.

16

TRIUMPH TO BETRAYAL

Jesus did not turn His back on the difficult task which was before Him. He and His disciples made the journey towards Jerusalem. When they came near the Mount of Olives, Jesus called two of His disciples over.

'Go to that village over there,' He said. 'You will find a young ass tethered. It has never been ridden before. Untie the animal and bring him to Me. If anyone asks you what you are doing tell them that the Lord needs this colt.'

The two disciples found the colt exactly as Jesus had described, tied outside a house. The owners did indeed ask what they were doing. But the answer, 'The Lord needs him,' satisfied them fully.

The men brought the colt back to Jesus. They threw their cloaks on the colt's back and helped Jesus on to his back.

As Jesus rode along the way some of them laid their coats on the road. Others cut down branches from the trees nearby and spread them on to the road.

On the road winding down the side of the Mount of Olives, the disciples began to shout and sing praises to God. The crowd of people following joined in too.

'Hosanna to the Son of David,' they cried. 'Blessed is the King that comes in the name of the Lord.'

Jesus rode into Jerusalem hearing the shouts

f triumph and praise from His disciples and others.

Not everyone was pleased. Some of the church leaders in the crowd demanded that Jesus would tell His disciples to be quiet. But Jesus refused.

'It is right that they shout out their praises,' He said.

Two days later many of the church leaders met with Caiaphas, the high priest. They plotted together to kill Jesus. One of the twelve disciples, Judas Iscariot, came to this meeting and offered to help them catch Jesus.

'What are you willing to give me?' he asked. 'I will give Him over to you.'

So they agreed to give Judas thirty pieces of silver if he would betray Jesus. From then on he was on the lookout for a chance to turn Jesus over to His enemies.

Jesus knew what was in Judas' mind. During the last supper with the disciples, He told them, 'One of you shall betray Me.'

The disciples naturally wanted to know who was about to do such a dreadful thing.

'Lord, tell us who it is,' said one. 'It is the man,' replied Jesus 'to whom I shall give this piece of food.'

He took the bread, dipped it in the dish and handed it to Judas Iscariot.

Immediately Judas left the room and went out into the dark night.

Jesus ate the supper with His disciples. He

spoke with them for many hours, warning them of difficult days ahead. Peter boldly said that he would never let Jesus down.

Jesus sadly said, 'Before the cock crows twice tomorrow morning, you will have denied three times that you know Me.'

Later that night Jesus went out to the Garden of Gethsemane to pray. Jesus often went there with His disciples. Judas knew that this was a favourite place.

Judas came to the garden with a large mob of men armed with swords and other weapons. They had made a plan together.

'I will point out Jesus to you by giving Him a kiss,' agreed Judas.

Jesus knew what was to happen. He bravely approached the crowd.

'Who are you looking for?' He asked.

'Jesus of Nazareth,' they replied.

'I am He,' stated Jesus simply.

Judas and the men were amazed and frightened by Jesus' straight reply. Judas carried out the arranged plan by greeting Jesus with the treacherous greeting 'Hail, Master' and giving Him a kiss. The soldiers then caught hold of Jesus, tied Him up and led Him away. The disciples left Him and ran away. How the circumstances had changed from His triumphant entry into Jerusalem a few days before.

17

DENIED AND TRIED

The band of soldiers led Jesus away to the palace of Caiaphas the high priest. There He endured a mockery of a trial. Many witnesses were brought to speak against Him. They told lies. Their statements did not agree.

'Tell us', demanded the high priest, 'whether You are Christ, the Son of God.'

Jesus answered, 'You have said it.'

The high priest was shocked. 'He has spoken blasphemy. We need no more witnesses.'

They spat in His face and slapped Him with their hands, mocking and jeering Him.

Peter and another disciple followed Jesus to the high priest's palace. A fire was burning in the middle of the courtyard and Peter sat among the people who were warming themselves in the chill of the early morning. A young girl who worked as a doorkeeper at the palace recognised Peter.

'This man was with Jesus too,' she said.

'Woman, I do not know Him,' snapped Peter. He moved out to the porch, just as the cock was

first crowing.

After a little while another person saw him and said, 'Aren't you one of them too?'

'Man, I am not,' denied Peter. 'I do not know this man.'

An hour later someone else said confidently, 'I am sure this man was also with Jesus. He is a Galilean too, he speaks like that.'

Peter replied in a panic, 'I do not know what you are talking about.'

Just at that moment the cock crew for the second time.

The Lord Jesus turned round and looked at Peter. Peter remembered what Jesus had said, 'Before the cock crows twice you will deny Me three times.'

Peter went outside and wept bitterly.

Jesus was tied up again and taken to Pilate, the governor of the land.

'What accusation do you bring against this man?' asked Pilate.

'This man is very bad,' they said 'We would not have brought Him here otherwise. He says things against our nation. He says He is Christ, a King.'

'Take Him away', said Pilate to the Jewish leaders, 'and judge Him by your law.'

'No' they replied, 'we could not sentence Him to death.'

Pilate went back into the hall, and called Jesus to him.

'Are You really the King of the Jews? Your own people, the Jews, have brought You to me. What have You done?'

Jesus replied, 'My kingdom is not worldly.'

'But are You a King?' retorted Pilate.

'You can say that I am a King,' stated Jesus. 'The whole purpose of My life in this world is to tell people the truth.'

Pilate then went out of the hall to the Jewish throng outside and said, 'I do not find Him guilty of any crime.'

The people would not accept this statement, but shouted out their objections. 'He is a troublemaker. He stirs up the people. He was always preaching His doctrine throughout the land.'

Pilate then tried to pass the responsibility on to Herod the king who was in Jerusalem at that time. Herod was very pleased to see this man Jesus about whom he had heard so much. Perhaps he would see some miracle from Him.

He questioned Him again and again, but Jesu remained silent. Herod and his soldiers mad fun of Jesus and sent Him back to Pilate.

Pilate called the chief priests and rulers an told them plainly, 'I have examined this ma and I found no fault in Him. Herod sent Hir back to me, so he could not have found any fau either.' Then he added, 'There is a custom tha a prisoner is released at this time of the Passove Feast. Will you allow me to release Jesus, th King of the Jews?'

'No,' they shouted. 'Not this man. Releas Barabbas.' Barabbas was a murderer and robbe

reason. Nothing would persuade them.

Eventually he gave in to their demands. He listened to the rabble rather than to his own conscience.

He took some water and washed his hands.

'I am innocent of killing this good man,' he said.

He foolishly thought that washing his hands would cleanse the guilt of his part in handing Jesus over to the soldiers.

The soldiers took Jesus and stripped off His clothes and put on Him a royal robe. They made a crown of thorns and pushed it on His head. They put a reed in His hand, like a sceptre. Then they pretended to bow down to Him, making fun of Him, then punching Him. Still Pilate insisted weakly, 'I find no fault in Him.'

The chief priests and officers shouted out, 'Crucify Him, crucify Him.'

'Take Him away yourselves and crucify Him,' suggested Pilate, 'for I cannot find Him guilty.'

'By our law He must die, because He says that He is the Son of God and no man should say that,' they claimed.

When Pilate heard this, he was even more afraid.

In the end the wicked men had their way. Pilate was not strong enough to stand up to them.

Jesus was led away to be crucified.

who was now in prison for his crimes.

'What will I do to Jesus?' asked Pilate.

They all said, 'Let Him be crucified.'

Crucifixion was a very slow and painful way to die, nailed on to a wooden cross.

Pilate tried once more to reason with them, but again the shout was to crucify Jesus.

'I will punish Him and let Him go,' Pilate tried again.

But the cry was even stronger. 'Release Barabbas. Take this man away. Crucify Him. Crucify Him,' they chanted.

For a third time Pilate appealed to their

18
CRUCIFIED

Jesus was led away from Pilate's hall. He was made to carry the large wooden cross to Calvary just outside the city wall. There Jesus was nailed to the cross by His hands and feet, and left hanging there in terrible pain until He died several hours later.

His suffering and death were fulfilling a wonderful plan of salvation for His people. All sin deserves to be punished. By suffering and dying for the sin of His own people who trust in Him, Jesus took the full punishment for all their sins.

What love He showed. Even when the men were nailing Him to the cross, Jesus prayed to God, 'Father, forgive them for they do not know what they are doing.'

The soldiers took Jesus' garment and cut it up into four parts. Each of them took a piece. His coat was made of one complete piece. 'Let's not tear it up,' said one of them. 'Let's cast lots and the winner can take it all.' Even that small detail had been foretold in the book of Psalms, many years before. Jesus' mother Mary and some other women were standing near the cross, watching what was happening. Mary must have been heartbroken. Even during His pain Jesus noticed His mother and His disciple John. Jesus said to His mother, 'Look on John as your son now.'

To John He said, 'Treat Mary like your mother.'

From then on John took Mary into his own home to look after her.

Two other men were crucified at the same time as Jesus, one on either side of Him. Both were thieves. One of the thieves complained to Jesus, 'If You are Christ, why can't You save Yourself and us.'

The other one was indignant.

'How can you speak like that?' he said. 'We deserve all this punishment but this man has done nothing wrong.'

Then he turned to Jesus and said, 'Remember me when You come into Your kingdom.'

'Today you shall be with Me in heaven,' Jesus assured him.

This man had believed in Jesus even at the end of his life.

He was completely alone.

When He called out, 'I am thirsty!', He was given a sponge soaked in vinegar.

After Jesus had drunk some vinegar, He called out, 'It is finished!' then with a loud voice, 'Father, into Your hands I commend My spirit.'

He then bowed His head and died.

At that moment the curtain in the temple was torn in two from top to bottom, the earth trembled, the rocks split open and some graves were opened.

When one soldier saw all this happening, he was very afraid.

'Certainly, this man was the Son of God,' he confessed.

Then the soldiers came to take the bodies of Jesus and the thieves down from the crosses. First of all they broke the legs of the two thieves to make sure that they were dead. When they saw that Jesus was already dead they did not break His legs. But one of the soldiers took his spear and thrust it into Jesus' side. Out poured blood and water.

That evening a rich man called Joseph went boldly to Pilate and asked if he might have Jesus' body to bury Him in his own tomb. His request was granted so Joseph, helped by Nicodemus, took Jesus' body from the cross and wrapped it in a linen cloth. They carried the body through a garden and laid it carefully in the tomb which was a cave and then rolled a big stone over the mouth of the cave.

The chief priests and religious leaders remembered that Jesus had said He would rise from the dead on the third day. They reminded Pilate of this. 'Give orders that the tomb is made very secure until the third day,' they said, 'just in case His disciples come and steal His body and say He is risen.'

'Go,' said Pilate, 'and make it as secure as you can.'

So the stone was specially sealed in front of the guard.

After being on the cross for six hours, Jesus reached the depths of His suffering.

He called out to God, 'My God, My God, why have You left Me?'

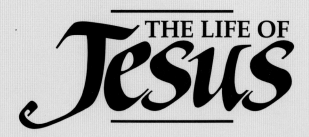

THE LIFE OF Jesus

LOOKING FORWARD TO GLORY

The adventures of Jonah are very exciting. The story was meant to teach a valuable lesson about Jesus. Jesus explained that just as Jonah was inside the whale for three days and three nights, so Jesus Himself would be three days and three nights in the grave. **(Matthew 12.40).** After that He would rise from the dead.

This wonderful fact is also referred to in **(Psalm 16.10).** The Holy Son of God would not be left in the grave.

Where is Jesus now?

19
HE IS NOT HERE; HE HAS RISEN

Very early in the morning of the first day of the week, Mary Magdalene and two other ladies came to the tomb where Jesus had been buried. They wanted to anoint Jesus' body with spices. On the way they discussed the big problem they were expecting.

'How are we going to get the stone rolled away from the front of the tomb?' they asked one another.

When they reached the tomb they were surprised. The stone had been rolled away already. Mary Magdalene rushed off to find Peter and John.

'Someone has taken away the Lord's body, and I do not know where they have put Him,' she said.

The other two ladies meantime crept right into the tomb. There they saw two men in dazzling white clothes - angels of the Lord. The women were very frightened.

'Do not be afraid,' said one angel. 'I know you are looking for Jesus, who was crucified. He is not here. He has risen from the dead on the third day. Go and tell His disciples, especially Peter, that He has risen from the dead.'

Peter and John came running when they heard the news from Mary Magdalene. They looked into the tomb and saw the linen graveclothes lying where Jesus had been. Peter and John went back home wondering at all the things that had happened.

Mary Magdalene came back to the garden. She was weeping with sorrow because she thought that Jesus' body had been stolen. A man came to speak to her.

'Why are you crying?' he asked. 'Who are you looking for?'

She thought this man was the gardener. She said, 'Sir, if you have taken Him away, please tell me where you have laid His body.'

The man said to her, 'Mary!'

She then realised that the man was the risen Lord Jesus.

'Master!' she cried out.

Mary and her two friends brought word to the rest of the disciples but they found it very hard to believe that Jesus was alive.

That same day, Cleopas and a friend were walking from Jerusalem to Emmaus, about seven miles away. All along the road they discussed the amazing happenings in Jerusalem in the past few days.

Jesus Himself came along beside them and walked with them. But they did not recognise Him.

'What have you been speaking about?' He asked them.

'Don't you know what has been happening in Jerusalem these past few days?' demanded Cleopas amazed.

'What things?' replied Jesus.

'The things that happened to Jesus,' answered Cleopas. 'The chief priests and rulers condemned Him to death and crucified Him. We had hoped that He would be the Saviour of our people. Three days have passed since His death. Some women went early to His tomb but they found it empty. Angels told them that He was alive. Some others of our friends went to the tomb, but they did not see Jesus at all.'

Jesus gently rebuked the men. 'You are so slow to believe what has been told you by the prophets. Christ had to suffer all these things before He entered glory.'

Jesus then explained to them all the Old Testament Scriptures which referred to Himself.

When they came to Emmaus, Jesus seemed to intend carrying on further.

They begged Him, 'Please stay with us. It is late now.'

Jesus went into the house with them and sat down for supper. He took the bread, blessed it and broke off a piece for each of them.

Only then did they recognise the risen Lord Jesus. Immediately He vanished from their sight.

'That explains how we felt as He spoke to us on the road, explaining the Scriptures to us,' they said to each other.

With no delay they walked back to Jerusalem to share their wonderful news with the eleven disciples.

'The Lord is risen indeed.'

20

BREAKFAST WITH JESUS

Some time later, Peter, James and John and several other disciples were together by the Sea of Galilee.

'I am going to go fishing,' said Peter.

'We will come too,' said the others.

But that night they caught no fish.

Just at daybreak they made for the shore again. They noticed a man standing on the beach.

He called out to them, 'Have you anything to eat?'

'No,' they replied.

'Throw your net over the right side of the boat; you will find fish there.'

They did as He said and the catch was so large that they could not pull the net into the boat.

John then realised that the man on the beach was Jesus.

'It is the Lord,' he gasped.

When Peter heard this he pulled on his coat and jumped into the sea to rush to the shore as fast as he could.

The other disciples followed in the boat, dragging the net with the great catch of fish.

When they all reached the shore, there was a fire lit, with fish already cooking and bread too.

Jesus invited them to bring some of the fish that they had caught too.

'Come and have something to eat,' He said.

Nobody had any doubts about who He was. They all knew that He was Jesus.

21

TAKEN UP TO HEAVEN

The risen Lord Jesus was seen and recognised by many people during the forty days that He lived on the earth after He was raised from the dead. He used this time to instruct His followers.

'Go into all the world,' He told them, 'and preach the Gospel to everybody.'

He led them out of Jerusalem to the Mount of Olives, near Bethany.

'I will send the Holy Spirit to help you and you will be My witnesses in Jerusalem, and Judea and Samaria, right to the furthest corner of the earth.'

As He said these words, He lifted up His hands and blessed them. His body was then lifted up from the ground and soon a cloud hid Him from sight.

The disciples stood gazing up to the heavens where Jesus went. Then two angels in white stood beside them.

'Why are you standing here, looking up to heaven? Jesus who was taken up into heaven will one day return in the same way.'

The disciples worshipped God and went joyfully back to Jerusalem to start the work that Jesus had set for them - preaching the good news of the Word of God.

Jesus is alive today. He is in heaven but He knows everything that happens to us here in the world. He cares for us and is continually praying to God the Father for His people.

The details written in the Bible about Jesus are there so that we may believe on Him and have Him as our Saviour and friend.

63

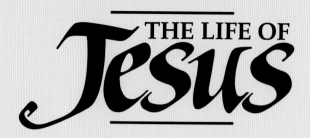

THE LIFE OF
Jesus

LOOKING FORWARD TO HIS RETURN

One day everybody in the world will realise that Jesus is the Lord. They will bow their knees to Him and say:

'Jesus Christ is Lord.'

On that day, sometimes called the Day of Judgement, Jesus will return. Those who do not care about Jesus will be sent away from Him. Those who love Him will be brought to Heaven to be with Jesus Himself.